Steve Preda

Summit OS
A Fable

One
Business's
Journey to the
Top of the Mountain

©2024 by Steve I. Preda

All rights reserved. No part of this publication may be reproduced, stored in a retrieval system, or transmitted in any form or by any means electronic, mechanical, photocopying, recording, or otherwise, without the written permission of the author, except for brief quotations in critical reviews and certain other non-commercial uses permitted by copyright law.

For permission requests write to: steve@stevepreda.com.

All persons mentioned with their written consent. All other characters are fictional and any resemblance to real persons is purely coincidental.

ISBN: 978-1-964710-05-1 (hardcover)
ISBN: 978-1-964710-04-4 (paperback)
ISBN: 978-1-964710-03-7 (e-book)

Amershire Publishing, Glen Allen, Virginia

Printed in the United States of America

Cover Design: Zoltan Ember

Text Design and Illustrations: Steve Preda and Zoltan Ember

Summit OS® is a registered trademark of EntrepCoach LLC, doing business as Summit OS Group.

ALSO BY STEVE PREDA

Buyable: Your Guide to Building a Self-Managing, Fast-Growing and High-Profit Business

Pinnacle: Five Principles that Take Your Business to the Top of the Mountain (with Gregory Cleary)

Strategy OS: Implement an Advanced Business Operating System in Six Simple Steps

DEDICATION

To clients and friends who trusted me to help them build well-oiled machine- and buyable businesses, and to those that allowed me to try.

Contents

Hacked	1
Stretched	3
Unicorn	5
In Denial	9
Reckoning	15
Summit OS	19
Right People, Right Seats	25
Tough Decisions	31
Unearthing the "Why"	35
Fresh Challenges	41
Meetings and Metrics	45
At the Precipice	49
Marching Towards a Vision	53
Stepping Up Rock Setting	59
Private Equity Adventures	63
Reframing the Climb	67
Turning the Tide	73
Sealing the Future	79
Epilogue: A New Horizon	83
What is Summit OS?	87
The 15 Business Growth Practices	89
The Author	93
Summit OS Group Trademarked Terms	95

Hacked

The ball celebrating high-end dermatology clinic Dexter Davis & Associates was buzzing with excitement. Balloons bobbed at every corner, and laughter filled the air as staff mingled, celebrating the opening of their new head office in downtown Austin.

Dexter, the charismatic founder, was the life of the party. Dressed in a sharp sports jacket and chinos, his peppercorn hair perfectly styled, he moved through the crowd with an ease that belied the undercurrent of stress he carried.

Lou Legstrong, the tech leader of DDA, navigated through the crowd, his face pale and expression grave—a stark contrast to the festivities. He finally reached Dexter, who was in the midst of sharing a laugh with a couple of his senior staff.

"Dexter," Lou called out, slightly out of breath. "We need to talk. Now."

Dexter's smile faded slightly as he noticed the urgency in Lou's tone. "Sure, Lou. Let's step into my office."

Inside the quiet office, Lou wasted no time. "It's the appointment system. It's been hacked. All appointments for the next twelve months—canceled."

Dexter's face drained of color. "What? How? Do we know who did it?"

"We don't, but that's not the worst part." Lou's hands trembled slightly. "When we tried to contact patients to reschedule, many had already booked with a new service—home visits from a competitor we didn't even see coming."

The news hit Dexter like a physical blow. He sank into his chair, the implications spinning through his mind. Financial disaster wasn't just a possibility; it was imminent.

"This can't be happening," Dexter muttered, rubbing his temples. "Did Karola hear about this?"

"Not yet. I came straight to you."

Dexter stood abruptly. "Keep this between us for now. I need to think."

Stretched

A month earlier, the Davis's spacious bedroom was a contrast of calm before the storm of their professional lives. Dexter and Karola were getting ready for the evening, each moving around the room with practiced ease, the air filled with the soft scent of perfume and anticipation.

"You know, Karola," Dexter began, adjusting his tie in the mirror, "this past year has been incredible for us. Opening those two new branches... it's more than I dreamed we'd accomplish so quickly."

Karola, choosing earrings, glanced at his reflection, a slight crease of concern marking her usually composed features. "Yes, it's been quite the year. But, Dexter, don't you think we're moving a bit too fast?"

Dexter turned to look at her directly, his expression one of mild surprise. "Too fast? Karola, this is what we've worked for. You saw the numbers yourself. Everything's aligning perfectly."

Karola nodded slowly, clasping her necklace. "I know, I know. The numbers don't lie. It's just..." She paused, searching for the right words without dampening his spirit. "It's a lot, and sometimes, big leaps come with big risks."

Dexter walked over and took her hands in his. "I understand your concerns, love. But remember when we started? How we promised we'd make this big? I couldn't have done any of this without you. This is our moment to shine, to really set our mark."

Karola smiled, her love for Dexter clear in her eyes despite her reservations. "Okay, let's go bigger then. How about we throw a grand office party to celebrate? Let everyone know that DDA isn't just growing, it's leading."

"That's the spirit!" Dexter's face lit up with his characteristic ambitious glow. "And I've been thinking of expanding further. Maybe hiring more specialists, perhaps even poaching a few stars from the competition."

Karola raised an eyebrow, her pragmatic side flickering to the surface. "Poaching, Dexter? That's aggressive. It could stir up some animosity, you know."

Dexter's grin didn't wane. "In business, it's about making bold moves. We need the best to be the best. Let's show them how serious we are. As for the party, spare no expense. Make it a night to remember."

Karola chuckled, her earlier reservations fading under his infectious enthusiasm. "All right, Mr. Davis. A night to remember, it shall be."

As they left their bedroom, the couple shared a look of mutual understanding and determination, unaware of the consequences their ambitious expansion would soon invoke.

Unicorn

For DDA's launch party, Blanton Museum of Art had been transformed into a venue of celebration and ambition. Dexter Davis stood on a small stage set against a backdrop of contemporary art, his audience filled with employees, patients, and friends. The room hummed with anticipation as Dexter, a champagne glass in hand, prepared to unveil his vision for the future of Dexter Davis & Associates.

"Ladies and gentlemen," Dexter began, his voice ringing clear and confident through the room, "tonight isn't just a celebration of what we've achieved. It's a promise of what is yet to come. We are not just expanding—we are revolutionizing the field of dermatology."

Applause broke out, led by Mac Middlehurst, the fractional CFO, whose eyes gleamed with the reflection of future profits and growth. Beside him, Marge Soldier, patient coordinator clapped, though her smile was tinged with concern.

Dexter continued, his demeanor that of a man who had never faced a setback he couldn't overcome. "Our plan is to go nationwide, setting up corporate offices and partnering with local dermatologists to perform our patented treatments. We're not just going to be the best in the country—we are going to crush any competitor who stands in our way."

The room erupted in cheers, Dexter's charisma casting a spell of invincibility over the crowd. Mac leaned over to Marge; his voice full of excitement. "Can you imagine? A Unicorn. An IPO on the New York Stock Exchange. This is the big leagues!"

Marge nodded, but her voice carried a note of caution. "It's ambitious, Mac. But don't you think it's a bit... fast? I mean, we're talking about a massive expansion in a very short time."

Mac waved off her concerns with a laugh. "Marge, when you have a leader like Dexter, you don't question the pace—you keep up. He's got a vision, and it's going to make us all very wealthy."

On stage, Dexter was reaching the climax of his speech. "I promise you, to everyone here who is part of this journey, you're not just building a career. You're building a legacy. You'll see riches beyond your wildest dreams."

As the crowd cheered, Dexter's eyes met those of his wife Karola across the room. She was smiling, her applause enthusiastic, but her eyes mirrored the hesitation that Marge felt. Their shared glance was brief but loaded with unspoken words.

After the speech, as the group mingled, Dexter, buoyed by adrenaline and applause, approached Karola and Marge, who were conversing quietly.

"Dexter, that was quite the speech," Karola said, her tone supportive yet cautious. "But are we ready for this? It's a huge step."

Dexter's smile didn't waver. "Karola, we've never been more ready. This is our time. Fear won't hold us back. We're going to do this, and we're going to succeed spectacularly."

Marge chimed in; her voice respectful yet firm. "It's not about fear, Dexter. It's about being prudent. Expansion is great, but the pace of it should be sustainable. We need to ensure we're not stretching too thin."

Dexter's gaze hardened slightly, a flicker of irritation showing. "Marge, I appreciate your concern, but I know the waters we're navigating. We need to be aggressive, or we'll be swallowed up by those who are."

Karola gently touched Dexter's arm, sensing his growing defensiveness. "She's not questioning your leadership,

Dexter. We all believe in you. It's just that... well, sometimes the best captains still need to listen to their crew."

Dexter took a deep breath, his initial irritation softening under Karola's touch. "Alright, I hear you both. But I'm telling you, this is the path to our future. Trust me, we're going to look back on tonight as the moment everything changed for us—for the better."

As the party continued, Dexter's words hung in the air, a blend of promise and pressure. Karola and Marge exchanged another glance, their smiles masking a shared concern about the thin line between bold leadership and reckless ambition.

This moment, filled with Dexter's confident declarations of a bright, unstoppable future, would soon be remembered not just for its optimism but for the dramatic challenges it foreshadowed, testing the resolve, loyalty, and wisdom of everyone in Dexter Davis & Associates.

In Denial

The evening air was brisk as Dexter and Karola hailed a cab outside the venue of their once jubilant party, now tainted by the shadow of the cyber-attack. As they settled into the back seat, the city lights flickered past, casting fleeting glows on Dexter's sullen expression.

Karola, ever observant, broke the silence first. "Dexter, talk to me. You've been quiet all evening, and I know it's not just exhaustion. What's going on in that head of yours?"

Dexter leaned back, staring out the window, his mind racing. "I'm fine, Karola. Just tired, that's all." His voice was strained, unconvincing even to his own ears.

Karola turned towards him, her tone gentle yet firm. "Dexter, we've been through too much for you to start hiding things from me now. This hacking incident... it's bad, isn't it?"

He sighed, the façade of indifference crumbling. "Yes, it's bad. But we've handled challenges before. We'll handle this one too."

"But this feels different, doesn't it?" Karola pressed, her worry evident. "This isn't just about lost appointments, Dexter. It's about trust—our patients' trust, our staff's trust. If we don't manage this right, it could change everything."

Dexter's denial clashed with the creeping reality. "We'll fix the systems, reassure the patients. It's just a setback, Karola."

Karola watched him, her eyes reflecting the streetlights. "A setback? Dexter, this could potentially ruin us. And it's not just about the business. What about the staff? Marge, Mac,

Lou... they rely on us. On this. We need to be open with them, with each other."

Dexter turned to face her, irritation mixing with desperation. "What do you want me to say, Karola? That I'm scared? That maybe I pushed too hard, too fast? Yes, I wanted to expand, to be the best, to never have to worry about money like I did when Mom... when we lost her."

Karola reached for his hand, squeezing it gently. "I know, love. I know how hard you've worked, why you've pushed. But sometimes, slowing down isn't a sign of weakness. It's wisdom. We need to think about not just growing, but sustaining."

Dexter's resistance waned under her compassionate gaze. "I just don't want to let anyone down. Not you, not our kids, not our team. I thought I was doing what was best."

"And you have," Karola reassured, her voice soft but steady. "You've built something amazing. But it's okay to be vulnerable, Dexter. It's okay to admit when we're out of our depth. Maybe it's time we sought more help from others who've been through this."

Dexter nodded slowly, the fight draining out of him as he considered her words. "Maybe you're right. Maybe I've been so focused on climbing that I didn't see the potential falls. I just... I don't want to go back to those days when we had nothing."

Karola smiled sadly, understanding all too well the fears that haunted him. "I don't either. But I'd rather face challenges with you openly than watch you struggle alone. Let's tackle this together, like we always do. We'll talk to the team, be honest about the situation, and make decisions together. It's not just your burden, Dexter. It's ours."

As the cab pulled up to their apartment building, Dexter felt a weight lift slightly. The road ahead was uncertain, fraught with challenges, but with Karola by his side, he felt a renewed sense of resolve. "Together," he echoed, a faint smile breaking through the turmoil. "Let's do this together."

Stepping out of the cab, they faced their building, a symbol of all they had achieved and all they stood to lose. But within them stirred a stronger resolve, a partnership that had weathered storms before and would do so again, no matter the odds.

ooooooooo

The next morning, when Dexter arrived at the office after his morning swim, he found Karola and Lou waiting for him.

"We need a strategy," Dexter announced as they gathered in the conference room. "And fast."

Karola, ever pragmatic, began, "First, we need to secure our systems. Lou, what are our options?"

Lou nodded, already a step ahead. "I'm on it. I propose a complete overhaul of our cybersecurity measures and possibly bringing in a consultant."

Dexter agreed, but his mind was on the bigger picture. "We need to understand this competitor. Who are they? How did they set up so quickly to capitalize on our misfortune?"

Karola, who had been quiet, finally spoke. "It feels orchestrated. The timing is too convenient. Dexter, I think this is an inside job or someone who knows our operations well."

The thought had crossed Dexter's mind too, but hearing it aloud from Karola made it all the more real and frightening.

Marge Soldier, knocked and entered with a worried look. "Dexter, several patients have called this morning. They're upset about the cancellations and are considering the new service. We need to do something."

Dexter pinched the bridge of his nose. "Thank you, Marge. Let's prioritize communication. Reassure our patients that we're fixing this, and maybe offer incentives to stay."

Marge nodded; her expression determined. "I'll draft something up right away."

As she left, Mac Middlehurst, walked in, his usual calm demeanor replaced by concern. "Dexter, we need to talk numbers. This hit could bleed us dry in less than six months if we don't stem the tide."

Dexter sighed. "I know, Mac. We may need to pull some emergency funds or look into a loan."

Mac frowned, his strategic mind racing. "I'll start reviewing our assets and credit lines. But we need to think about long-term survival."

The morning wore on, filled with discussions and plans. Yet, despite the strategies, the threat loomed large, an unseen yet pervasive enemy that had shaken the very foundation of Dexter's empire.

By late afternoon, Dexter felt the weight of their situation more acutely than ever. He needed guidance, a fresh perspective. That's when he remembered Fletcher Henson, a seasoned business coach known for turning crises into opportunities. The two of them have been members of the same YMCA for years, and have become friends.

He picked up the phone and dialed. "Fletcher, it's Dexter Davis. I need your help."

Reckoning

Back in the present day, as the revelations of the hacking scandal sank in, Dexter couldn't help but recall their conversation from a month ago. His drive to expand had indeed brought unforeseen risks into sharp, painful focus.

Sitting across from Fletcher Henson, Dexter's usual confidence was undercut by a visible strain. Fletcher, who carried an empathetic yet firm demeanor, listened intently as Dexter outlined the situation.

"Fletcher, we've been hit hard. Our systems, our appointments, compromised. And there's this competitor, Derma Tech International—suddenly everyone's talking about them. They knew exactly when to strike."

Fletcher stroked his beard thoughtfully. "It sounds like you've been blindsided, Dexter. But let's consider all angles here. Expansion can often leave gaps in your defenses, not just in security but in loyalty too. Tell me about this competitor. Any idea who's behind it?"

Dexter leaned back; frustration evident in his furrowed brow. "No names yet. But the timing, just as we were pushing forward... it feels personal."

Fletcher nodded. "It often is, in cases like these. Now, tell me about your team. Anyone new who might have had the access and motive?"

Dexter hesitated, his thoughts going to the recent hires, the ambitious expansion, the so-called poaching of talent. "We brought in a lot of new faces, particularly from competitors. You think it could be an inside job?"

"It's a possibility we can't ignore," Fletcher advised, his voice steady. "But our focus needs to be dual-tracked. Secure what's been compromised and regain the trust of your team and patients. Dexter, this is a wake-up call, not just to tighten your security, but to really assess the culture you've cultivated."

Dexter sighed, the weight of responsibility settling on his shoulders. "I've been so focused on growth, I might have overlooked... perhaps, the foundation."

"That's what we need to strengthen," Fletcher affirmed. "And it starts with transparency and communication. Have you spoken to your team about this openly?"

"Not in detail, no." Dexter admitted, realizing his mistake. "I wanted to protect them, to handle it at the leadership level."

Fletcher leaned forward, his gaze intent. "Dexter, people rally when they feel part of the solution. It's time to bring them into the fold, show them that their leader is human but resolute. Vulnerability can be a powerful tool for unity."

Dexter nodded, a plan beginning to form. "I'll call a meeting. Lay it all out. It's time they knew exactly what we're facing."

"And what about Karola?" Fletcher's question was pointed. "How is she handling this? Her perspective could be invaluable."

Dexter's expression softened. "Karola's been my rock. But I know she's worried, more about the people we might let down than the business itself. She's always seen the heart in our operations."

"Good," Fletcher smiled slightly. "Lean on that. Her empathy with your drive can create a balance you're going to need going through this storm."

As Dexter left Fletcher's office, he realized the true test of his leadership wasn't how he celebrated the highs, but how he navigated through the lows. With Fletcher's guidance, he was ready to face his team, not just as their boss, but as their leader, one who was finally ready to lead from the front, vulnerabilities, and all.

oooooooooo

Back at the office Dexter sat across from Mac Middlehurst, whose usual calm demeanor was replaced by a grim expression as he shuffled through the financial reports spread out between them.

"Dexter, we need to talk about our financials," Mac began, his voice steady despite the troubling news he was about to deliver. "The hacking incident has accelerated issues that were already under the surface due to our rapid expansion. Our revenues have plummeted faster than we projected."

Dexter leaned forward, clasping his hands together on the desk. "Give it to me straight, Mac. How bad is it?"

Mac took a deep breath, his eyes not leaving the papers. "If we don't implement a significant restructuring immediately, we might be weeks away from bankruptcy."

The words hung heavy in the air. Dexter blinked, shock momentarily overtaking his usually unshakeable composure. "Weeks? But the expansion, the investments in new offices—were they all for nothing?"

"It's not just the expansion," Mac continued, his tone meticulous and factual. "It's the increased overheads, the new hires, the advanced tech. We stretched too thin, too fast. And now, with the revenue drop due to the hacking, our cash flow is critically tight."

Dexter's mind raced, his ambitious plans clashing violently with this new reality. "So, what are you saying? That we pull back? Close offices?"

Mac looked up, meeting Dexter's gaze firmly. "I'm saying we need to consider all options. Layoffs, downsizing, maybe even selling off some assets. It's about survival now, Dexter, not expansion."

Dexter rubbed his temples, feeling the weight of each word. "I promised them, Mac. I promised our team—riches, stability, growth. How do I go back on that now? How do I tell them that their trust in me... might have been misplaced?"

"It's not about misplaced trust," Mac reassured, leaning forward. "It's about adapting. Every business faces trials. It's how we respond that defines us. You're a visionary, Dexter, but every visionary needs a realist to keep things grounded. That's what I'm here for."

Dexter sighed, his initial resistance giving way to reluctant acceptance. "Okay, let's say we do this—restructure, cut costs. How do we even begin to decide what and who goes?"

Mac pulled up a spreadsheet on his laptop, pointing to various figures. "We start with non-essential expenditures. Then we look at our least profitable offices. As for staff, we keep those essential for day-to-day operations and those who are critical for what DDA stands for—top-notch patient care and innovation."

Dexter nodded slowly; the path forward daunting yet clear. "And what about the morale? This will hit everyone hard. I need to be honest with them, don't I?"

"Yes, transparency is crucial," Mac agreed. "But it's also about framing. This isn't just cutbacks; it's strategic realignment. You're not just saving money; you're saving the company, their jobs, their future."

Dexter stood, pacing slowly by the window, looking out over downtown Austin. "I've always been the one with the plan, the next big step. Now, I need to be the one to hold things together."

Mac watched him, respect mingling with concern. "You can do this, Dexter. You've led us here; you can lead us through this. It's about showing that you care not just for the success of DDA but for everyone who makes it what it is."

Turning back from the window, Dexter's gaze was resolute. "Alright. Let's draft up the changes. I'll speak to the team. They deserve to hear it from me, firsthand."

Summit OS

The downtown YMCA in Austin was a sanctuary for many, its lanes a place for clearing minds and pushing physical limits. Today, however, Dexter found neither peace nor relief as he aimlessly swam in the central lane, his strokes more erratic than the thrashing thoughts swirling in his mind. His company's dire financial situation mirrored the chaotic splash with each stroke, disrupting the smooth rhythm of other swimmers around him.

A stern voice cut through the sound of splashing water. "Sir, you need to keep to one side! You're disrupting the other lanes!" shouted the pool warden, a lean man with an authoritative tone, standing at the edge of the pool.

Flustered and embarrassed, Dexter tried to apologize, but his words were drowned out by the swim master's continued admonishments. Just then, Fletcher Henson walked into the aquatic area. Recognizing Dexter's distress, he quickly approached the warden.

"Jim, let me handle this, please," Fletcher said calmly, gesturing with reassurance. The pool warden nodded stiffly, stepping back to allow Fletcher to take over.

"Dexter, come on out. Let's talk in the sauna; you look like you could use some warmth and a quieter space," Fletcher suggested with a gentle pat on Dexter's shoulder.

Gratefully, Dexter followed Fletcher to the sauna, wrapping a towel around his waist and settling onto the wooden bench. The heat of the room enveloped him, a stark contrast to the cold dread that had chilled him since his meeting with Mac.

As they sat in the soothing warmth, Dexter sighed deeply. "Fletcher, I'm at a loss here. We're on the edge of bankruptcy, and every move now feels like it could be our last."

Fletcher listened intently, his expression one of focused concern. "I understand, Dexter. It's a critical time, but it's also an opportunity to steer back with a solid strategy. I've been helping other business owner clients with something that might just be what DDA needs."

Dexter looked up; interest piqued despite his despondence. "Oh? What's that?"

"It's called the Summit Operating System™, or Summit OS® for short," Fletcher began, his voice reflecting his passion for the subject. "It's based on the book, *Pinnacle: Five Principles that Take Your Business to the Top of the Mountain*. It's a holistic approach to business management, focusing on core areas that align with your company's needs right now."

Dexter leaned forward, the warmth seeping into his muscles, easing some tension. "Tell me more about these principles."

Fletcher nodded, outlining the system. "First, we focus on People – engaging your team, creating clarity of culture and function ownership and leadership development. Then comes Purpose – Articulating your company's energizing higher purpose, its "Why". We have to then set clear and attainable goals that align with your Company Why™ and which unite your people. Next is Performance – improving how these goals are achieved with structure and gamified accountability.

Then, Playbooks come next – defining and ingraining best practices that create efficiency and consistency, to scale the business. Lastly, Profit. Dexter Davis & Associates must develop Unique Activities that will differentiate you and make you highly and sustainably profitable."

The 5 Business Growth Principles™

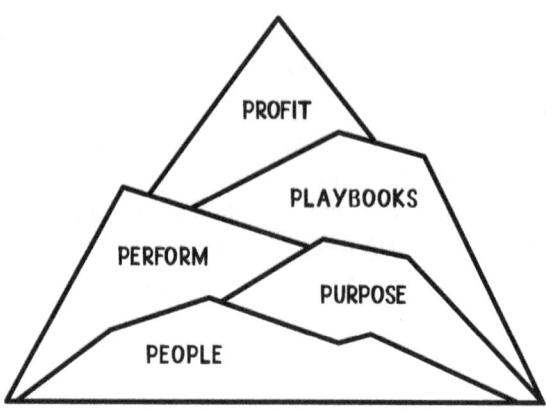

Dexter absorbed the information, a spark of hope flickering in his weary eyes. "It sounds comprehensive. But how do we implement something like this with everything already so unstable?"

"That's where I come in," Fletcher assured him, his tone confident. "I help you apply these principles, step by step. We'll start with workshops for you and your leadership team, assess where adjustments are needed, and begin the realignment."

Dexter nodded slowly, the sauna's heat finally thawing his chilled spirits. "It sounds like exactly what we need. Something to pull us together and focus on climbing out of this hole."

"Exactly," Fletcher agreed, standing as they prepared to leave the sauna. "And I'll be with you at every step. We'll start first thing tomorrow. Ready to start the climb, Dexter?"

With a deep breath, Dexter stood, a newfound resolve steeling his features. "Ready as I'll ever be. Let's take DDA to the top of the mountain, Fletcher."

As they left the sauna, the weight on Dexter's shoulders felt lighter, knowing he had a seasoned guide in Fletcher. Together, they prepared to navigate the treacherous business terrain that lay ahead, armed with Summit OS and a renewed determination to save Dexter Davis & Associates.

○○○○○○○○○○

After their sauna discussion, Dexter and Fletcher walked across to Houndstooth Coffee on Congress Avenue, a spot known for its robust brews and artisan sandwiches. The casual setting was a stark contrast to the tension Dexter carried with him, despite the promising strategy Fletcher had laid out.

As they ordered their coffee, Fletcher noticed the slight furrow on Dexter's forehead, a sign he was deep in thought or concern. "You seem a bit on edge, Dexter. What's on your mind?"

Dexter took a deep breath, accepting his coffee from the barista with a nod of thanks. They found a quiet corner, the hum of the coffee shop creating a discreet backdrop for their conversation. "It's this whole Summit OS rollout. I know it's what we need, but I'm uneasy about opening up to the team about how bad things really are."

Fletcher sipped his coffee, giving Dexter a moment to organize his thoughts. "It's natural to feel vulnerable in these situations. But transparency can be a powerful tool for rallying your team. They need to see the real picture to understand the stakes and the necessity for change."

Dexter played with the sleeve of his coffee cup; his discomfort palpable. "It's more than just being open about the numbers, Fletcher. It's about admitting that my decisions led us here. And the dynamics... they're not as healthy as they could be. Despite our successes, there's been tension, competition... I've overlooked a lot in the pursuit of growth."

Fletcher nodded, understanding the complexity of Dexter's position. "Unhealthy dynamics can fester, turning small cracks into dangerous chasms under pressure. This is your chance to address and mend those rifts. What specifically concerns you about the team's morale?"

Dexter sighed; the weight of leadership heavy on his shoulders. "There's been a lot of one-upmanship, especially among the newer executives who were part of our aggressive expansion. It's created cliques and some resentment. And with the recent bad news, morale is at an all-time low. Everyone's on edge, wondering about job security, their future."

"Those are significant challenges," Fletcher acknowledged, "but also opportunities. Summit OS will help reorient these dynamics toward a more cooperative and mission-focused model. Part of this process will involve leadership training, rebuilding trust, and aligning everyone's efforts towards common goals rather than individual agendas."

Dexter absorbed Fletcher's words, a mix of apprehension and resolve on his face. "And how do we begin this transformation? How do I start this conversation without losing their confidence entirely?"

Fletcher set his coffee down, leaning in with a focused gaze. "We start by setting up a meeting with your leadership team. Introduce them to Summit OS as a new beginning, a chance to reset and move forward together. But you lead with your vulnerability. Show them that you're human, that you recognize the issues, and you are committed to change. Your openness will encourage them to trust the process—and you—more deeply."

Dexter nodded slowly, the advice settling in. "That's going to be one of the hardest things I've ever done, Fletcher. But you're right. If I expect them to buy into this new direction, I have to be the first to take that step."

"Exactly," Fletcher said, a reassuring smile on his face. "I'll be there with you, every step of the way. We'll plan this meeting together, outline the key points of Summit OS, and prepare you to address the tough questions."

Finishing his coffee, Dexter nodded: "Thanks, Fletcher. Let's get that meeting scheduled. It's time to turn things around, no matter how tough it's going to be."

Right People, Right Seats

In a nearby Hampton Inn conference room, the Leadership Team assembled for a crucial workshop led by Fletcher Henson. Today was Base Camp Day 1™ of the Summit OS Journey and the agenda was focused on redefining the organization's core values and restructuring their functional leadership—both necessary steps to recover from recent setbacks and stimulate growth.

The morning sunlight filtered through the blinds, casting long shadows across the table where Dexter, Fletcher, Mac, Lou, Karola, and Marge sat with notes and laptops ready. Fletcher opened the session with a clear, motivating tone. "Today, we rediscover what made DDA successful and realign our functions around these core values. Each of you will play a pivotal role in this transformation."

Dexter nodded, feeling a mix of anticipation and anxiety. He knew the importance of today's decisions for the future of DDA. "Let's start by identifying the behavior-based core values that drove our growth to five locations in just a few years," he suggested, looking around the table for input.

Karola, who virtually ran the office, and was always pragmatic and insightful, was the first to speak. "One of our strengths has always been our patient-centered approach. We need to ensure that remains a core value."

Marge, the patient coordinator, agreed, her voice filled with passion. "Empathy and care are what our patients praise most. These should be at the heart of our values."

Lou, still smarting from the hack but eager to contribute, added, "Efficiency in our processes and innovation in our services have also been key. We need to retain those."

As they discussed, Fletcher guided them to refine these ideas into clear, actionable core values. "Most companies misfire with this exercise when they define ideals their organization should stand for, which I call "corporate values", rather than behaviors and mindsets they can hold their team accountable to." - He said.

Corporate vs. Core Values

CORPORATE VALUES vs. Core Values	
INTEGRITY	"Tells the Truth"
PROFESSIONALISM	"Respects Others"
TEAMWORK	"Has Your Back"

Source: Steve Preda, Gregory Cleary: *Pinnacle: Five Principles that Take Your Business to the Top of the Mountain* (Amershire Publishing, 2022)

"The former tend to be big words with multiple meanings, such as 'Integrity', 'Professionalism' and 'Teamwork'. However, it is more helpful to pick behaviors, such as 'Tells the Truth', 'Respects Others' and 'Has Your Back' and hold everyone in the company accountable to them.

The team synthesized the 27 values they brainstormed into five phrases that captured the essence of DDA's culture: Honest with Empathy, Listens to Understand, Wills to Win, Commits to the Team, and Strives to Improve.

Along the way, Fletcher helped them steer clear of Patrick Lencioni's famous value traps and avoided picking table stakes, aspirational or incidental values.

Core Value Filter™

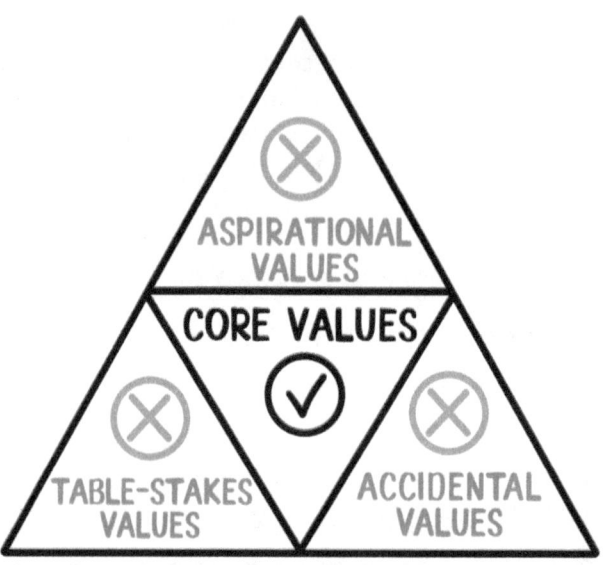

Source: Steve Preda, Gregory Cleary: *Pinnacle: Five Principles that Take Your Business to the Top of the Mountain* (Amershire Publishing, 2022)

With the core values set, the next step was to define the crucial functions of DDA that needed attention to move the practice forward. Fletcher explained, "Think of yourselves as Mini-CEOs™ of these functions. Each of you will develop the vision for growth and impact for the function you own, aligned with our soon-to-be defined company vision."

The room vibrated with energy as the team brainstormed the critical functions. They identified Sales, Patient Care, Technology, Finance, and Practice Management, and the CEO role as areas needing focused leadership.

Mac, the fractional CFO took ownership of the Finance function. "I'll focus on restoring our financial health with precise Budgeting and new Funding Strategies," he declared, already thinking about the numbers. The team brainstormed:

Insurance/Billing, Payment/Collections, and Payroll as other outcomes Mac would be responsible for.

Lou, needing a redemption arc after the cybersecurity fiasco, was reinforced as the owner of Technology. "I'll ensure our systems are not only secure but also cutting-edge," he asserted, determined to regain his colleagues' trust. The outcomes the team defined for his function included: Device Management, HIPAA Compliance, Pharmacy Integrations, Cybersecurity and Software Development.

Marge was affirmed as the owner of Patient Care, drawing on her natural empathy and extensive experience. "I want to ensure every patient interaction reflects our core values," she said, her determination clear. The team picked Consultations, Scheduling, Procedures, Pre-Op Care and Post-Op Care, as critical outcomes to focus on.

Karola, though initially quiet, spoke up about the importance of staff development. "Our employees are our greatest asset. I'll work on aligning their growth with our goals and values," she stated, her voice steady and confident. The group unanimously thought her to be the right person to own Practice Management.

The Function Ownership Chart™ of Dexter Davis & Assoc.

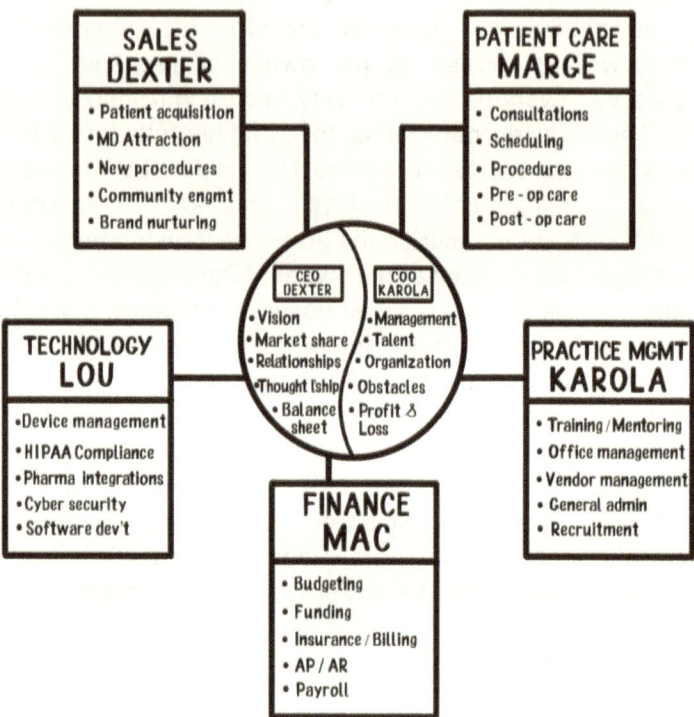

Inspired by: Steve Preda, Gregory Cleary: *Pinnacle: Five Principles that Take Your Business to the Top of the Mountain* (Amershire Publishing, 2022)

Practice management would shine if Training and Mentoring, Office Management, Vendor Management, General Administration and Recruitment were taken care of- They thought.

Finally, Dexter led the discussion, focusing on the crucial outcomes for DDA's Sales Function. He emphasized the importance of patient acquisition, noting its proven impact on revenue. Mac agreed, highlighting that attracting top dermatologists would enhance the clinic's credibility and attract more patients.

Dexter then shifted the focus to introducing new procedures to stay ahead in the competitive market, which Marge supported, pointing out their value in keeping patients engaged and drawing in those seeking the latest in care.

Karola interjected, reminding everyone of the importance of community engagement and brand nurturing. She suggested more proactive involvement in the community through wellness events and skin care seminars to bolster DDA's presence as a caring and integral part of the local scene.

Dexter wrapped up the meeting by integrating these insights into their sales strategy, tasking Karola with ramping up community events and Marge with ensuring patient communications reflected these innovative changes. The team agreed to focus on creating an ecosystem where their brand could thrive on innovation and trust.

Tough Decisions

With the future-shaping Functions assigned, Fletcher introduced an exercise called Talent Assessment: We will now map how each individual at DDA is aligned around Core Values and consistently delivering on the critical Outcomes we entrusted them with.

"Your A-players and A-potentials, or "Climbers" exhibit your core values and perform consistently well." – Said Fletcher, explaining the top right quadrant of the Talent Assessment Matrix. They are the people to look after, as they strive to grow themselves, as well as your business.

"Who are the Campers and the Cranks?" Interjected Marge, pointing at the chart Fletcher just sketched on a yellow 3M flip chart. "Aren't the B-players or Campers being some of our favorite colleagues who are however not pushing the envelope?" Inquired Lou. "Yes." Affirmed Fletcher. Lencioni often calls them 'lovable slackers'". "They are great to go camping with as long as all we want them to do is entertain us around the fire. Unfortunately, you'll be stuck erecting tents and cooking dinner yourself.

"I think we have at least a couple of "Cranks," whom I think would be in the B/C quadrant." Said Mac. "Jason and Tracy, for example, are highly competent coders, but they can be insufferable. No one wants to work with them, and they don't seem to mind."

"They are hard-workers for sure, but they prefer to work in their cocoons and dislike taking input from other departments. Their 'we-know-best' attitude may have contributed to our cybersecurity lapses." Acknowledged Dexter to Lou's visible consternation.

"At least we have no Cavemen, who are both unliked, and ineffective" Added Karola with a sigh of relief. "Unless they are hiding in a cave, unbeknownst to us" said Lou to lighten the mood and distract from the criticism of his team.

The assessment was revealing. Using the criteria Fletcher outlined, they categorized their 22 employees as A-, B-, and B/C-players. This exercise, though difficult, was necessary to understand where their team stood.

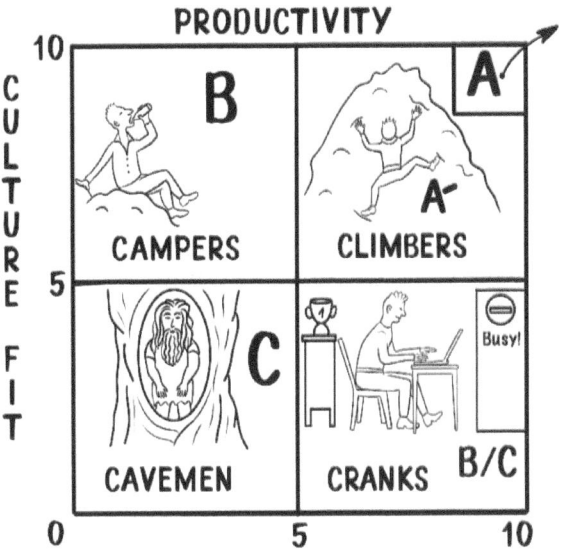

Inspired by: Steve Preda, Gregory Cleary: *Pinnacle: Five Principles that Take Your Business to the Top of the Mountain* (Amershire Publishing, 2022)

As they discussed the results, Dexter brought up a sensitive issue. "We have identified three high-paid employees who fall into the B and B/C-player categories. Given our current financial strain, we cannot afford to keep them."

The room tensed at the implication of letting people go. Lou looked uncomfortable, rubbing the back of his neck, while Marge frowned, clearly worried about the impact on morale.

Fletcher sensed the rising discomfort and steered the conversation. "These are tough decisions, but necessary for our survival. Each role must contribute effectively to our recovery and growth."

Dexter, seeing the need for further sacrifices, made another, more personal appeal. "I'm asking everyone here to take a 20% pay cut to help turn our ship around. I'll be doing the same."

This request sparked a heated debate. Lou, his pride still bruised, responded half-heartedly, "If it's absolutely necessary, I'm in, but I want to see clear results from these changes."

Marge, ever the advocate for the team, was reluctant. "It's a big ask, Dexter. Everyone is already stretched thin. How can we ensure this will lead to a turnaround?"

Dexter acknowledged her concerns. "I know it's a lot to ask, but we need everyone to pull together. These cuts are temporary, and with the plans we're putting in place, I believe we can come out stronger."

After much discussion, the group, though still apprehensive, endorsed Dexter's plan. They agreed on the importance of shared sacrifice to navigate through the crisis.

As the meeting broke for lunch, the team felt a mixture of apprehension and resolve. They had started charting a new path forward, one that required personal sacrifices and a commitment to revitalizing DDA's core values.

Walking out of the conference room, Dexter felt the weight of the leadership mantle. He wondered how he could forge the necessary unity and resilience in his team, in the face of this rising challenge.

Unearthing the "Why"

Dexter Davis and his leadership team reconvened after a brief lunch break. The atmosphere was charged, a blend of apprehension and the lingering energy from their earlier decisions about restructuring and pay cuts. Today's afternoon session, guided by Fletcher, would start with Karola delving into the emotional core of Dexter Davis & Associates —the Company Why of their practice.

Fletcher, initiated the session with a calm, compelling tone. "This afternoon, we're going to explore the deeper purpose of our work here at DDA. Understanding why we do what we do will not only guide our business strategies but also reconnect us with our passion for our work."

The team, though initially skeptical about another emotionally charged exercise, began to warm up to the idea as Fletcher prompted them to think about the impacts of the services of Dexter Davis & Associates on their patients' lives.

After 15 minutes of brainstorming Marge, driven by a deep-seated belief in patient care, quipped: "We're not just in the business of treating skin conditions. We help people feel confident in their skin, maintaining healthy and attractive appearances as they age."

Her words resonated around the room, and one by one, other team members chimed in with personal stories of patients whose lives had been dramatically improved through their care. Lou, typically reserved, shared a particularly touching story about a young man whose severe acne was cured at DDA, and how his thus increased confidence transformed his social life and self-esteem.

"Helping people maintain healthy and attractive skin into old age," Fletcher summarized, capturing the essence of their shared sentiments. "That's a purpose that can drive us, that can inspire our strategies and our everyday interactions with patients."

The "Why" of Your Business

```
                    Co.
                   WHY

         /\
        /  \
       /SUMMIT\
      / VISION \
     /----------\
    / MT MILESTONES\
   /   STRATEGY    \
  /ANNUAL GROWTH PLAN\
 /   S.T.E.P. ROCKS   \
/    WEEKLY METRICS    \
/     DAILY ACTIVITIES   \
```

Inspired by: Steve Preda, Gregory Cleary:*Pinnacle: Five Principles that Take Your Business to the Top of the Mountain* (Amershire Publishing, 2022)

The room, previously tinged with the stress of compensation cuts, now buzzed with renewed purpose and excitement. The team felt a collective surge of motivation to propel DDA towards recovery and growth.

With the Company Why clearly defined, Fletcher steered the session towards setting financial metrics and establishing what he called "Sprint Rocks"—initiatives that each team member would focus on to drive the most critical outcomes for their respective functions in the first thirty days.

As they delved into this task, however, old tensions began to surface. Mac, focused intensely on cost management, clashed with Lou over the allocation of resources for upgrading cybersecurity measures. "We need to be prudent with every dollar we spend," DDA's finance chief argued, his voice firm and unwavering.

Lou, feeling cornered but determined, retorted, "What's the point of saving money if we leave ourselves vulnerable to another attack? We need to invest in robust tech to protect our future."

Sprint Rocks

Fletcher observed the exchange quietly before intervening. "Let's remember our Company Why. Every decision we make—whether it's financial austerity or technological investment—should support our core mission of helping people maintain healthy skin."

The discussion around "Sprint Rocks" continued, with each member defining their critical tasks for the following four weeks. Karola, ever the advocate for patient experience, committed to overhauling the appointment scheduling system to reduce wait times and improve patient satisfaction.

As the day drew to a close, Fletcher introduced the concept of Daily Standup Meetings, a practice met initially with groans around the room. "Another meeting?" Marge questioned, her tone a mix of fatigue and skepticism.

Meetings and their Purposes

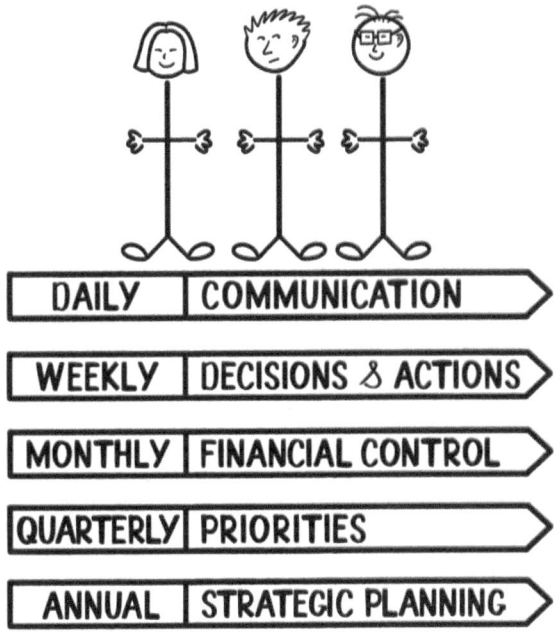

Fletcher smiled, understanding their reluctance. "Think of it not as just another meeting, but as a vital check-in. It's about keeping our lines of communication open, sharing updates, and addressing needs promptly. Just five to ten minutes each day where we discuss what happened yesterday, what will happen today, and where anyone might need help."

"This meeting is about communications. I will show you how to use other meetings to focus on accelerating decisions, controlling your finances, setting priorities, and performing strategic planning, respectively, in our upcoming sessions." Fletcher explained for context.

The idea, once fleshed out, began to make sense to the team. They agreed, albeit somewhat reluctantly, to start the next morning with their first Daily Standup Meeting. Fletcher assured them, "This will enhance your ability to respond quickly to emerging challenges and break down siloes between functions. Having a touchpoint on your calendar will also cut down on one-on-one check-ins and eliminate noise, helping you all focus better for the rest of the day."

"What will be our next steps?" Inquired Dexter.

"We'll populate a Summit OS Portal™ for you, in the next 24 hours, with your Function Ownership Chart, Company Why, Sprint Rocks and meeting timer so that you can run your Daily Standup Meetings™, and I will be checking in with the team regularly to make sure you are executing." Responded Fletcher.

The session ended on a note of cautious optimism. The team had not only clarified their operational priorities but had rediscovered the emotional heartbeat of their practice. As they filed out of the room, there was a sense of clarity and a flicker of hope—a shared belief that a turnaround for DDA was not just necessary, but imminent.

Dexter lingered behind, reflecting on the day's accomplishments. The alignment of strategy with passion, the commitment to improved communication, and the palpable dedication of his team filled him with a resolve he hadn't felt in months. As he turned off the lights and closed the door, he felt ready to face whatever challenges lay ahead, bolstered by a team that was more united than ever in its mission to help people maintain beautiful, healthy skin into old age.

Fresh Challenges

On a balmy Friday evening, the leadership team of Dexter Davis & Associates convened at their cherished local sports bar, launching what was quickly becoming their second favorite pastime—morale-boosting team dinners. Dexter had whipped up this new tradition not only to foster camaraderie but also to offer a brief respite from the ceaseless office grind.

"These daily standup check-ins are not quite as painful as I feared," Lou quipped, nursing his drink with a grin. "I dreaded starting the day with a call, but it actually helped me keep a pulse on what's going on. Plus, the tech team felt more in the loop about our hacking crisis, which surprisingly boosted morale—go figure!" He chuckled, raising his glass in a mock toast to the situation.

Karola, leaning in from across the table, chimed in with a smile, "And I truly appreciated Mac's financial updates. It's a relief to know someone else is carrying that burden. Honestly, it's like having a financial weather forecast—mostly cloudy with a chance of bankruptcy!" Her comment drew a round of laughter from the table, lightening the mood as they all shared a knowing look.

As laughter and lively discussions filled the air, the sudden switch of the television to a news channel grabbed everyone's attention.

The headline on the screen read, "Congress approves radical Medicare changes. Cuts funding for 'unproven' dermatology protocols." The news was a severe blow—many of DDA's most profitable procedures were now deemed 'unproven' and would not be covered by Medicare. The team's initial shock quickly turned to concern as they absorbed the potential impact on their practice.

Lou, usually reserved, couldn't hide his frustration. "It's just another example of how disconnected the policymakers are from the realities of medical practice," he said sharply, his mind racing with the implications for the technology upgrades he had championed.

Marge, sitting beside Dexter, felt a knot form in her stomach. Her visceral commitment to patient care, rooted in her early experiences watching her mother manage a small clinic, made her particularly sensitive to changes that could affect patient access. "This could make it difficult for many of our patients to afford the treatments they need," she said quietly, her voice tinged with worry.

"We have our work cut out for tomorrow," Dexter sighed, referencing the upcoming morning session with Fletcher scheduled in DDA's office for the next day. Mac, always the strategist, had suggested they all meet on a Saturday. "It saves us the rent at the Hampton Inn, and ensures no office crises can disrupt us," Mac pointed out pragmatically.

The mood had decidedly shifted. The team finished their meals in a more subdued manner, the weight of the news curtailing the evening's earlier cheer.

Unbeknownst to them, further troubles were on the horizon...

○○○○○○○○○○

Early next morning, Dexter's heart sank as he read an email from his attorney detailing a new lawsuit against DDA—a patient had alleged that a failure to diagnose their cancer's metastasis had led to preventable complications. The legal and reputational risks were enormous. Gathering his resolve, Dexter immediately called Fletcher to warn him before their full day leadership team session scheduled to start at 9 am.

By the time Fletcher walked into DDA's conference room, the atmosphere was tense. The team was gathered, their expressions ranging from worried to defiant.

"Let's focus on what we can control," Fletcher began, trying to instill a sense of purpose. "We need to understand how to function effectively under these new conditions, and that starts with clear communication and accountability."

Dexter nodded, appreciating Fletcher's direct approach. "We've been through tough times before," he said, looking around the table. "Each challenge has pushed us to innovate and improve. This time will be no different."

Meetings and Metrics

Fletcher introduced the concept of Weekly Tactical Meetings. "These will be crucial for navigating the upcoming changes," he explained. "They will focus on Peer Accountability for our metrics and 'Sprint Rocks,' helping us identify and solve problems quickly."

Marge, who had always prioritized patient care above all, felt a growing unease. "I'm concerned that in our rush to address these financial issues, we might sideline what really matters—patient care," she voiced her worry, her experience in hospice care making her acutely aware of the human cost of such decisions.

Dexter turned to Marge, understanding her fears. "Your dedication to our patients is exactly why we need your input in these meetings, Marge. We have to balance the books, yes, but not at the expense of our core mission."

Karola chimed in, supporting Marge. "Dexter's right. These meetings aren't just about cutting costs. They're about ensuring we continue to provide the best care, in the most sustainable way possible."

Lou, still skeptical about the bureaucratic hurdles, added, "We need to be agile, yes. But let's not forget that the technology and systems we put in place are fundamental to our operational efficiency."

The discussion that followed was intense. The team delved into the specifics of how they could use their new tactical meetings to not only track financial metrics but also to ensure that patient care standards were not compromised.

Fletcher guided them in setting up a structure for these meetings that would allow for effective problem-solving, making decisions and assigning Action Items.

"Did you say we would also be defining Metrics today?" Dexter asked, turning to the coach. Fletcher rotated his flip chart to display headings: Function, Owner, Outcomes, Metric, and Target/Week. "Yes, indeed. Do you all remember how we defined the major Functions, the expected Outcomes for each, and appointed Owners, whom we called mini-CEOs during our Base Camp Day 1 meeting?" Henson queried the group.

"And how do we ensure everyone focuses on the 20% of activities that deliver 80% of the results for their Function?" he asked rhetorically. "We'll conduct a Scoreboard Sketcher exercise to identify one or two Metrics for each leadership Function to drive momentum. Metrics can measure outputs or drive inputs. We prefer to focus on inputs—those we control and which we believe will generate the desired outputs. If they don't, we tweak the Metrics until they do."

"We already measure data every month. Can we just use our existing KPIs for this exercise?" Mac interjected. Dexter responded, "I recommend measuring Metrics weekly. This will give us near real-time data on our progress. By the time we get monthly numbers, it might be too late to catch up with our quarterly financial targets."

"Can you give us a few examples, Fletcher?" Lou asked, always keen on the details. The coach started filling in the flipchart with examples from the book *Pinnacle: Five Principles*, guiding the team. "We like to gamify this exercise, aiming to hit two-thirds or three-quarters of the Metrics each week to win, which we call the WTW Scoreboard™."

The WTW Scoreboard of Dexter Davis & Associates

FUNCTION	OWNER	OUTCOMES	Metrics	TARGET/W	YES/NO
CEO	DEXTER	Thought Leadership	# of Videos and Blogs Published	>3	Y
		Big Relationships	# of Partners Engaged	>2	N
SALES	DEXTER	Patient Acquisition	# of New Patients Inquiries Received	>15	Y
		MD Attraction	# of Dermatologists Engaged	>3	Y
PATIENT CARE	MARGE	Scheduling	% of timeslots Filled - Next 30 days	>90%	Y
		Procedures	Average Treatement Time per Procedure	<20 mins	N
TECHNOLOGY	LOU	Software Development	# of Lines of Codes written per Day	>90	N
		Cybersecurity	Average Incident Response Time	<60 mins	Y
FINANCE	MAC	Insurance Billing	Insurance claims and bills issued < 3 days	>95%	Y
		Collections	Receivable Days	<30	Y
PRACTICE MGMT	KAROLA	Training & Mentoring	Number of Mentor Meetings Conducted	>1	Y
		Recruitment	Number of Candidates Engaged	>3	N
WON THE WEEK?				>=8	Y

As the meeting drew to a close, Fletcher emphasized the importance of Tackling Topics decisively. "The goal here is to increase our decision and execution velocity. We can't afford to be slow in adapting to these changes. By focusing on the discipline of identifying and addressing as many topics as we can and turning them into action, we can create a massive momentum from this crisis."

"At-risk Metrics and Rocks are good candidates to discuss, in addition to other problems or opportunities contributed by members of the group. Dexter, I recommend you canvass your leadership regularly for topics and add the ones emerging in the Daily Standup Meetings. Its best practice to prioritize Topics before you delve in and tackle them in order or importance." Explained the coach.

The team left the room with a mixture of resolve and apprehension. They had a plan, but the path ahead was fraught with uncertainty.

Dexter understood the delicate balance they needed to maintain between financial sustainability and patient care. The challenges were daunting, but he wanted to feel confident in his team's ability to navigate them.

As he turned off the lights and locked the conference room, he felt ready for the challenges ahead, bolstered by the unity and determination that had emerged from today's session.

At the Precipice

The news of the lawsuit had barely settled within Dexter Davis & Associates when another crushing blow threatened the stability of the practice. Dexter received an urgent call from Pillar Bank late one evening; the tone was somber and the message dire. The bank was calling in the loan used to finance their recent office buildout, citing a breach of covenant triggered by the legal and financial turbulence DDA was experiencing. The practice needed to come up with $2 million within three months to avoid facing bankruptcy.

Dexter felt the weight of the world on his shoulders as he hung up the phone. He knew that the next steps he took could very well determine the fate of his entire team and the patients they served. Without hesitation, he called Fletcher who was getting ready for their next full-day Summit OS session, he called Base Camp Day 2™.

The next morning, the DDA leadership team was back at the Hampton Inn making sure they would be able to work uninterrupted and away from prying eyes of colleagues. They wore expressions of concern mixed with determination. Henson, ever the calm in the storm, started the session with a level of urgency that matched the gravity of their situation.

As the group started checking in for the day, Mac Middlehurst, their finance czar, suggested the creation of a monthly cash flow projection. "We need to understand exactly where our money is coming and going every month. This will help us monitor our expenses rigorously and stay on budget."

Karola, whose strength lay in managing operations smoothly, added, "We should also establish the Monthly Financial Meetings™ Fletcher talked about last Friday at the bar. This way, we can keep a close eye on our financial status as a team and make regular adjustments, as needed."

Lou, normally reserved but now fully engaged given the stakes, proposed reaching out to private equity investors. "We have a solid business model and a good track record, despite recent events. There are investors who look for opportunities like ours to provide rescue financing."

The suggestion sparked a mix of hope and anxiety. Dexter knew that bringing in private equity could mean significant changes in how DDA was run, possibly even diluting his ownership. But the alternative was far worse.

After the excitement of the check-in died down, Fletcher stepped back in to progress the agenda.

"Today we need to address our financial emergency head-on," Fletcher announced. "We're going to establish a long-term ambitious goal we call Summit Vision™, Medium-Term Milestones™ to chart a vivid and credible vision towards it, and a high-level plan for the rest of the year which would drive our quarterly "S.T.E.P. Rocks™" going forward, which I'll explain later."

Then the coach revisited the five core values and the Company Why that the group had established four weeks earlier.

"We said our firm was, and will continue to be, built by people who are Honest with Empathy, Listen to Understand, Will to Win, Committed to the Team, and Strive to Improve," Fletcher recapped. "Then we said Dexter Davis & Associates exists for 'Helping people maintain healthy and attractive skin into old age.'"

"Are we sure we got our Core Values and Company Why right?" Fletcher asked, making eye contact with each team member, seeking either a nod of approval or a suggestion for improvement. "I think we nailed them all," Karola confidently asserted, with the team murmuring their agreement in unison. "People need beautiful skin, and we possess the right qualities to advocate for this cause," she added.

After a short break, Fletcher introduced the concept of the "Summit Vision," which was also termed "pinnacle" in the book of the same title. "The concept was most famously articulated by Jim Collins, who called it a Big Hairy Audacious Goal," he added.

"How does the Summit Vision relate to the Company Why?" Lou asked. "Aren't they the same thing?"

"Actually, they're often confused. For instance, some believe that John F. Kennedy's call to go to the moon was a 'Why' for the United States. But it was actually a Summit Vision, aiming towards the greater unstated Why of "demonstrating the supremacy of democracy over communism". The Company Why should be an enduring aspiration, something we strive towards by achieving multiple Summit Visions along the way" Fletcher explained.

"What are the criteria for a good Summit Vision statement?" Marge inquired.

"I'd think, in addition to being 'hairy and audacious,' it probably should also be specific and measurable?" Mac jumped in with a half-question, earning a nod of approval from Fletcher.

Summit Vision (big, long-term, measurable goal)

Inspired by: Steve Preda, Gregory Cleary: *Pinnacle: Five Principles that Take Your Business to the Top of the Mountain* (Amershire Publishing, 2022)

After gathering suggestions and engaging in a lively debate, Dexter proposed that the company should "10x its sales revenues in 10 years." This would be achieved through expansion across the country and continued innovation in skin care procedures and evolving DDA's proprietary digital platform.

"I love '10x in 10.' It has a nice ring to it," Lou supported the suggestion enthusiastically, and everyone approved. "Time for lunch," quipped Marge, whose blood sugar was dipping into hangry territory. It was indeed a perfect moment for a break, which the coach quickly granted. The delivery from Sweetgreen has just arrived.

Marching Towards a Vision

After a 30-minute lunch break everyone was back at their seat and Fletcher shared copies of a worksheet titled Milestone Mind-Juggler™. It was time to brainstorm a vivid vision three years out for Dexter Davis & Company. What would the firm look like at the end of the third fiscal year from now? What milestones would have to be accomplished along the way so that they would be well on their way to their 10-year Summit Vision?

    The Mind-Juggler Exercise was designed to trigger ideas around the 5 Business Growth Principles of: People, Purpose, Performance, Playbooks and Profit.

Milestone Mind-Juggler

PEOPLE	PERFORMANCE	PROFIT
• Team structure	• New Customer Acquisition	• Business-Line profitability
• Talent attraction	• New Sales Channels	• Client-level profitability
• Training & Development	• Growing Existing Customers	• Industry-elite profitability
• Culture strength	• Customer Concentration	• Continuous Improvement
• Best place to work	• Marketing Initiatives & Approaches	• Operational Excellence
• Owner-dependency	• Leverage Customer & Market Data	• Return on Equity
	• Market Awareness	
	• Thought Leadership	

PURPOSE (Strategy)	PLAYBOOKS
• Competitive Position	• Technology Tools & Initiatives
• Strategy Stack	• Systems & Processes
• Geographic Expansion	• Optimizing Playbooks
• New Verticals & Industries	• Process automation
• Innovation	• Single person dependency
• Acquisitions & Disposals	
• Business reinvention	

Fletcher helped the team synthesize their ideas down to the following Medium-Term Milestones.

- $10,000,000 in sales with $3,000,000 net profit
- 50 doctors supporting patients
- 15 offices around the country
- 100 hospitals are connected to our dermatology management platform
- Developed and launched our second proprietary dermatology procedure
- Best place to work award winner in five cities.
- All our Functional and Sub-functional Playbooks have been Defined, Ingrained and Optimized
- We have developed a patented bespoke patient experience

Medium-Term Milestones™

- All our surgical offerings are on the first page of Google's organic search rankings
- We are a top five US dermatology practice on Facebook, Instagram and YouTube

With the energy in the room still high from formulating the Medium-Term Milestones, Henson smoothly transitioned to the next crucial topic on their agenda: building an Annual Growth Plan for 202X. The team leaned in, ready to tackle the financial goals that would focus on overcoming the immediate challenges and stabilize DDA at the previous year's sales figure of $4,000,000 million, with an imperative to break even or better.

Annual Growth Plan

"We need to solidify our footing financially, ensuring that we maintain last year's sales while keeping our expenses in check," Fletcher began, setting the stage for a focused brainstorming session. "It's about stabilizing now so we can grow later."

The team nodded in agreement; each member acutely aware of the financial tightrope they were walking. Fletcher then distributed yellow sticky notes and Sharpies, energizing the atmosphere as each person began jotting down their ideas for initiatives that could help reach these goals.

"Think about what projects can directly impact our Sales, Patient Care, Technology, Finance, and Practice Management functions," Fletcher encouraged as the scribbling intensified. "These should not only aim at financial stabilization and maintaining revenue but should also pave the way towards accomplishing at least partially some of your Medium-Term Milestones."

As the sticky notes began to fill up the walls, the room turned into a hive of activity. Dexter walked around, reading over shoulders and nodding approvingly at the creative energy being unleashed.

Karola, always with an eye on operational practicality, suggested, "Let's categorize these into broader annual goals that can really mobilize everyone around the company. It's about creating a unified direction that all departments can rally behind."

Lou, tapping a sticky note onto the wall under 'Technology', chimed in, "I've got an idea for improving patient interface systems. It could reduce waiting times and boost patient satisfaction scores. Aligns perfectly with our desired outcomes for Patient Care and Technology."

Mac, focused on the financial aspect, added, "We should consider a thorough review of our expense management system. If we can cut down unnecessary expenditures, that directly contributes to our goal of not losing money this year."

Marge, who had been quietly observing, finally spoke up, "What about a community outreach program? It can help drive new patient visits and also strengthen our Practice

Management by showing we are committed to the community."

Fletcher gathered the team for a review of the collected ideas. "Let's thematize these into our broad annual goals. This way, we can start assigning teams and resources to each initiative effectively."

The group worked together, clustering similar ideas and identifying overlaps and synergies. As they grouped the sticky notes into coherent themes, a clear plan began to emerge, covering all key aspects of the business.

Dexter looked over the themed goals, a sense of pride welling up. "This is exactly the kind of collaborative planning we need. With these initiatives in place, I'm confident we can navigate through this year's challenges and set a strong foundation for the future."

Stepping Up Rock Setting

The prior week, Fletcher took the opportunity to observe and then critique how the team conducted their Weekly Tactical Meetings. He noticed that while the leaders appeared committed, there was a lack of clarity in how decisions were made and actions were prioritized. This was a good time to bring that up.

"To improve our weekly meetings, we need to start setting S.T.E.P. Rocks: Specific, Transparent, Elevating, and Periodic goals," Fletcher advised. "This means picking important goals, articulating them clearly, planning them precisely, and spreading out the execution steps effectively over the time period, which is typically a quarter, but may be as short as a month in a time of crisis like we are facing today."

"This approach will force you to think through necessary contributions from others and potential pitfalls, so that you can plan around them." The coach added. "You can have these Rock-Steps be owned by others on the team who will get a chance to approve or negotiate them in your first upcoming Weekly Tactical Meeting."

Implementing Fletcher's feedback, the team began to redefine their approach. The first order was to address the immediate financial crisis by solidifying their cash flow projections and setting up a stringent budget review process.

As the discussions unfolded, fierce disagreements emerged, particularly between Lou and Mac. Lou was focused on maintaining his tech advancements, while Mac was preoccupied with cutting costs wherever possible.

S.T.E.P. Rocks

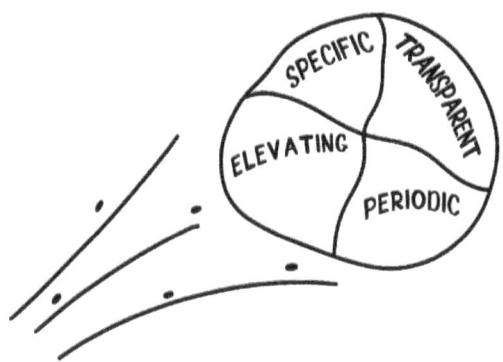

Inspired by: Steve Preda, Gregory Cleary: *Pinnacle: Five Principles that Take Your Business to the Top of the Mountain* (Amershire Publishing, 2022)

"Every dollar spent on tech is a dollar not stored for emergencies," Mac argued, his voice tense with frustration.

Lou countered, his frustration equally evident, "And every piece of outdated tech is a risk to our operations and security. We can't afford to be penny-wise and pound-foolish."

The tension in the room was palpable until Dexter stepped in. "Both points are valid," Dexter said, bridging the divide. "But right now, our priority must be survival. Mac, work with Lou to identify essential tech expenditures that align with our immediate financial goals. At the same time Frazer and I will start reaching out to private equity investors who may be interested to invest in our Company Why and "10x in 10" Summit Vision.

With Dexter's intervention, the team gradually aligned. They agreed to Fletcher's method of setting S.T.E.P. Rocks, which helped clarify their immediate and long-term objectives.

As the meeting drew to a close, the coach facilitated a commitment from each team member to take rapid action to stabilize the company. Everyone on the team owned one or two S.T.E.P. Rocks and they agreed to develop four to eight

Rock-Steps for each, spread as evenly as practicable over the next 90 days, until the first Quarterly Lookout Meeting™ of DDA.

Team members also agreed to execute one week Action Items for one-step activities that arose from the discussion. They agreed on individual responsibilities and on working arm-in-arm to steer Dexter Davis & Associates away from the brink of collapse.

As everyone left the room, there was a sense of cautious optimism. The path forward was fraught with challenges, but also lined with opportunities for growth and stabilization. Dexter conferred with Fletcher on the monumental tasks ahead. With the coach's guidance and the growing dedication of his team, he felt ready to face the challenges and save the practice that was their livelihood and their passion.

Private Equity Adventures

Five months later...

Dexter Davis and Fletcher Henson emerged from the gleaming downtown offices of Medical Growth Partners, their expressions painting a picture of contemplation with a hint of concern. They had just wrapped up their third investor meeting of the day, a critical moment in their pursuit to secure Dexter Davis & Associates' financial future.

Courting investors had proven to be difficult. Starting after Base Camp Day 2, Mac had diligently conducted an exhaustive search for private equity firms interested in medical practices, and Dexter had been tirelessly engaging them for months. After making over a hundred approaches and signing three dozen Non-Disclosure Agreements, they were now narrowing down the prospects to a select few firms still considering their proposal.

The day had started early with Dexter and Fletcher reviewing their presentation over dark roast drip coffee at a café near their first meeting location. Dexter, driven and ambitious, felt the familiar mix of nerves and excitement churn within him. He was passionate about DDA's mission to help people maintain healthy and attractive skin into old age, and he believed in his firm's growth potential despite the obstacles.

Fletcher's calming presence and strategic insights, reassured Dexter. Having turned businesses around before, including building and selling his own investment bank ten years earlier, Fletcher knew what these investors were looking for.

"Remember, it's not just about selling them on the numbers. It's about painting a compelling vision and building trust in our capability to navigate sector volatility," Fletcher advised as they prepared for the day.

Their first two meetings of the day, however, had not gone as hoped. The potential investors were initially intrigued but had expressed reservations by the end of their discussions. "They're concerned that the recent Medicare changes would diminish our profitability," Dexter shared, frustration lining his voice as they walked away from another fruitless presentation.

Fletcher nodded, processing the feedback. "It's a valid concern. But let's focus on how we can turn that around. We need to highlight not just how we've managed thus far but how we plan to adapt and thrive. Our next meeting could be the game-changer."

As they approached the third private equity firm's offices, Dexter took a moment to gather his thoughts. "This is more than just a pitch. It's about projecting a future where DDA leads the market. We've got the Company Why, the team, and the strategy. Let's make them see that."

Fletcher and Dexter stepped into their next meeting, ready to make a compelling case for investment. The stakes were high, but they were prepared to demonstrate that Dexter Davis & Associates would not just survive the industry's challenges but was poised to redefine them.

ooooooooo

The meeting with Medical Growth Partners was indeed different. Morgan Jones, a seasoned investor with an eye for potential, was curious about DDA's mission and Dexter's enthusiasm. Fletcher's background and his ability to articulate strategy and growth avenues impressed him too.

"Mr. Davis, Mr. Henson, I'm intrigued" Morgan began, leaning back in his chair. "Your Company Why resonates with us, and your track record, Fletcher, demonstrates expertise and a pattern of success that we look for in our partners."

Dexter nodded, encouraged by these comments. "Thank you, Mr. Jones. We are committed to not just sustaining but significantly expanding DDA's reach. We believe that with your partnership, we can achieve that."

Morgan's gaze was sharp, his mind processing every detail. "However," he continued, "the recent Medicare changes present a hurdle. How do you plan to pivot and differentiate DDA in this new environment? And more importantly, how will you execute your expansion strategy profitably?"

Fletcher took the lead on this, outlining their strategic initiatives including leveraging technology to improve patient engagement and operational efficiency. "Our plan includes targeted expansion into areas not affected by Medicare changes, diversifying our service offerings to include more self-pay procedures, and enhancing our cosmetic dermatology line," Fletcher explained.

Morgan listened intently but his expression remained non-committal. "And what about your team? For a plan of this magnitude, you'll need a cohesive and committed team. Our investment philosophy is focused on businesses that can realistically project a 5x growth in value over a five-year period. That's only possible with a compelling long-term vision and a believable medium-term plan with credible annual goals consistently executed."

The discussion that followed was intense. Dexter spoke passionately about his team, their skills, and their dedication. Yet, he knew that recent strains and the looming financial pressures have tested the team's cohesion and resolve.

As the meeting wrapped up, Morgan's parting words were both encouraging and daunting. "You have the beginnings of a compelling pitch. I see potential here, but I need to see more—more detail in your execution strategy and more evidence of your team's alignment and commitment."

Walking out into the cool afternoon air, Dexter and Fletcher were silent for a few moments, each lost in thought. The challenge laid out by Morgan was immense: to not only stabilize DDA but to grow its value fivefold in an uncertain healthcare landscape.

"Fletcher," Dexter finally said, his voice tinged with both determination and exhaustion, "we have our work cut out for us."

Fletcher nodded, his mind already turning over solutions. "Yes, we do. But Dexter, remember, every challenge is also an opportunity. We need to regroup, refine our pitch, and most importantly, ensure our team is fully on board and moving in the same direction. We can do this."

The ride back to the office was quiet but the resolve was building. They knew the task ahead was daunting, but the potential rewards for their patients, their team, and their practice were too great to ignore. Notwithstanding Fletcher's help and Summit OS, and the passion of his leadership team, is it even possible to flip their business and financial challenges into a new chapter of growth and success for DDA?

Reframing the Climb

The brisk December morning air nipped at the leaders of Dexter Davis & Associates as they congregated at a secluded conference center for a two-day strategic planning session. With the stakes at their highest, Fletcher Henson, their business coach, had outlined an agenda to transform their crisis into a growth opportunity.

"As we stand on the brink of a new year, it's crucial to reflect on our past several months," Fletcher began, scanning the room with a determined gaze. "Today, we'll review our achievements and draw lessons. Following that, we'll strategize and measure your progress towards the Summit. In the afternoon, we'll work on team cohesion. My goal is for all of you to leave this retreat not just as colleagues, but as a unified, trusting unit."

Everyone engaged in dissecting their financial results and annual goal completions alongside their quarterly progress.

"Your S.T.E.P. Rock process has shown remarkable improvement," Fletcher commended, nodding approvingly. "You've excelled in holding each other accountable and accomplishing all your quarterly priorities."

Mac, always keen on the details, chimed in: "We managed to stabilize the business and even achieve 3% revenue growth this year. Notably, half of our patients returned from Derma Tech International after realizing their approach lacked the personal touch we maintain here at DDA. Moreover, we've controlled costs effectively after the fallout, keeping DDA profitable for the year."

Karola, reflecting on the team dynamics, added, "It's not just about the numbers. Our unity and mutual support have been crucial. Every challenge we faced, we tackled together, and that's what brought many of our patients back. They trust not just our expertise, but our commitment to them as a team."

Lou, looking ahead, suggested, "Moving forward, we should capitalize on this momentum. Let's enhance our patient engagement strategies and continue improving our operational efficiency."

Marge, who had been meticulously taking notes, agreed, "I believe focusing on fine-tuning our patient outreach and care will be essential. It's about reinforcing why they chose us in the first place."

After lunch, Fletcher opened the session with an exercise he called "Facing Brutal Facts." It was designed to confront the harsh realities the business faced without succumbing to despair. The team could then prioritize initiatives to mitigate such challenges.

"Today, we begin by accepting our current reality, no matter how tough it is," Fletcher started, projecting a calm yet firm presence. "Only by acknowledging these brutal facts can we move forward effectively."

One by one, team members voiced the challenges: the hacking incident had exposed vulnerabilities in their IT systems; the Medicare changes threatened their core revenue streams; and the lawsuit could damage their reputation irreparably. Each admission was a painful acknowledgment of the threats looming over DDA.

However, Fletcher guided the discussion towards constructive outcomes, encouraging the team to identify immediate remedial actions for each challenge. Mac suggested further tightening financial controls and seeking alternative revenue sources. Lou committed to an accelerated cybersecurity overhaul. Marge focused on patient outreach to bolster DDA's reputation and counteract the negative publicity from the lawsuit.

As the discussion deepened, Dexter shifted the focus toward their long-term objectives with a note of urgency in his voice. "These suggestions are helpful, but to reach our Summit of 10x growth in 10 years, we need more than just incremental improvements. We have nine years to boost our revenues to 40 million dollars, and that won't happen by just working harder or cutting costs."

He paused, allowing his words to resonate with the team before continuing. "That's why I propose a fundamental shift in DDA's business model. We should move from an owner-centric 'brains model' to a more scalable 'efficiency model.' This approach would involve leveraging a robust group of employed doctors and an apprenticeship system. We'd also incorporate Physician Assistants and Nurses to build scale and save on costly salaries, while simultaneously attracting young medical talent eager to master our patented surgery methods."

His suggestion sparked immediate interest around the room, stirring a mix of curiosity and excitement as the team began to see the potential of such a transformative strategy.

oooooooooo

The second day's session focused on articulating updated medium-term milestones that would turn their new business model into reality, followed by a new Annual Growth Plan for the coming 202Y.

As the strategic planning session continued, Dexter gathered his team around a cluttered table filled with charts, graphs, and now, their new project—Playbooks for every Function within DDA.

Dexter started, his tone as serious as it was hopeful, "Alright team, we're moving forward with Defining and Ingraining our Playbooks. These aren't just documents; they're our blueprint for the future. We need these to not only create efficiencies but also to dazzle those private equity investors with the kind of profit margins they can't ignore."

Lou, always ready to lighten the mood, chimed in, "So, we're basically writing a bestseller for the business world? I hope it's more 'How to Succeed in Business' and less 'Surviving Apocalyptic Profit Margins.'"

Karola, flipping through a stack of notes, added, "Each Playbook needs to cover everything from how we greet patients to how we bill them without making it feel like a goodbye to their wallet. If we can Optimize and Automate processes, we can guarantee consistency and scalability—which, let's be honest, sounds less like healthcare and more like we're launching the next iPhone."

Mac, looking over the financials, couldn't help but weigh in, "And let's not forget the golden rule: if the Playbook doesn't help save money or make money, it's only going to be useful as a doorstop in our beautifully efficient, automated offices."

Marge, always the patient advocate in the room, pointed out, "We need to ensure these Playbooks keep the human touch in our patient service. It's great to be efficient, but let's not turn into robots. Unless, of course, Dexter is planning to unveil a line of doctor-bots as a surprise twist!"

Dexter laughed, appreciating the team's input and humor. "No doctor-bots, I promise. But seriously, great points everyone. These Playbooks are critical. They'll help us streamline operations and maintain the high standards our patients expect and deserve. Let's keep this energy up and make these Playbooks something we're all proud of."

The team nodded, their laughter mingling with a renewed sense of purpose as they dived back into the details of their ambitious plan.

As they wrapped up the planning session, Fletcher addressed another crucial element: team dynamics. The stress of their performance challenges had intensified interpersonal frictions within the team. To enhance understanding and cooperation among the team members,

Fletcher introduced an exercise based on a personality assessment team members completed as preparation for the session. Fletcher called the exercise "Cover Blindspots".

Each member shared insights from their respective DISC assessments, revealing their work styles, communication preferences, and leadership approaches. Dexter, a dominant leader, acknowledged his tendency to make rapid decisions, sometimes at the expense of team consensus. Karola, known for her stability and detail orientation in operations, admitted she could be resistant to abrupt changes.

The exercise was eye-opening, fostering empathy and better understanding among the team. Members provided constructive feedback on potential blind spots, helping each other see how they could become more effective leaders.

As the session closed, the team felt a renewed sense of unity and purpose. The challenges ahead were daunting, but the roadmap they had crafted gave them a clear direction. The strategic shift towards an efficiency model, underpinned by a solid plan for financial and operational restructuring, rekindled their hope and determination.

Driving back from the retreat, Dexter felt a mixture of relief and anticipation. The discussions over the past two days had not only strengthened their strategy but also their bond as a team. With Fletcher's guidance and the collective commitment of his leadership team, Dexter was confident that DDA was on its way to reaching its Summit, poised to transform its crisis into a legacy of success.

Turning the Tide

Dexter Davis stood before the partners of Medical Growth Partners with Fletcher Henson at his side, the fluorescent lights of the boardroom casting shadows across their determined faces. The air was thick with anticipation as Dexter launched into his presentation, outlining DDA's strategy for growth and financial sustainability.

Dexter: "Ladies and gentlemen, thank you for considering our vision. At DDA, we're poised to redefine dermatological care by leveraging our patented procedures and proprietary patient care process to drive both growth and profitability."

PE Partner 1: *(leaning forward skeptically)* "Mr. Davis, your vision is compelling, no doubt. However, we're concerned about the feasibility of achieving the profit margins you project without further dilutive capital raises. How do you plan to manage that?"

Dexter: *(confidently)* "We understand the importance of maintaining capital efficiency. Our model leverages an advanced operational framework that maximizes patient throughput while minimizing unnecessary expenditures."

PE Partner 2: "But based on your current numbers, even a slight underperformance could necessitate additional funding. How do you respond to that risk?"

The room filled with a tense silence as the partners awaited Dexter's rebuttal. Fletcher, sensing the need for a strategic pivot, interjected with a calm yet assertive tone.

Fletcher: "If I may, perhaps we could request a follow-up meeting? We have some refinements to our strategy that could address your concerns more directly."

PE Partner 3: "Alright, you have 10 days. Impress us, or we may need to reconsider our position."

As Dexter and Fletcher left the building, the weight of the task ahead was palpable. They needed a breakthrough strategy, and they needed it fast.

oooooooooo

Back at DDA headquarters, the leadership team convened around the expansive oak conference table for an urgent two-day strategy session. The atmosphere was thick with both apprehension and resolve as Fletcher outlined the agenda, emphasizing the need for a deep dive into financial restructuring. "We'll focus on developing an Advanced Profit Per X™ focus, a Strategic Flywheel™, and a unique Strategy Stack™ to secure the high and defensible margins we need," he explained.

Karola, always focused on streamlining operations, responded thoughtfully. "It's crucial that whatever model we develop, it must enhance our patient care. We cannot sacrifice quality for cost savings." Lou agreed, adding his perspective: "And from a tech angle, automating certain patient interactions without losing the personal touch could be key."

As the team brainstormed, Marge brought up a promising development involving Jonah, one of their engineers. "Jonah has developed a new non-invasive technique for skin analysis and he's close to patenting it." Dexter perked up at this news, intrigued. "How developed is his work?" he asked. Marge replied, "It's nearly market-ready. Integrating Jonah's technology could revolutionize our diagnostics and treatment tracking."

The discussion soon pivoted towards a new business model. Mac suggested moving to a franchise model, explaining: "Franchising could leverage our existing reputation and Jonah's innovation, allowing for rapid scalability without the hefty upfront investments of corporate-owned expansions." Fletcher nodded in agreement. "Each franchise could act as an entrepreneurial arm, adapting our outreach methods to local needs while adhering to our high standards. This could be a key part of our Strategy Stack."

Dexter Davis & Associates' Strategic Flywheel

Inspired by: Steve Preda: *Strategy OS: Implement an Advanced Business Operating System in Six Simple Steps* (Amershire Publishing, 2023)

The team then defined their Strategic Flywheel a concept from Strategy OS®, a sequel program to Summit OS, that allow businesses to develop highly profitable differentiation. Lou started outlining a potential cycle: "As per the model, our flywheel should start with the Advanced Profit Per X metric which we had identified in an earlier leadership session. We determined that our goal should be to maximize the value of our patient outcomes and therefore we picked: Profit per Patient Outcome."

"Growing our profit per patient outcome allows us to invest in developing advanced diagnostics, which boosts patient satisfaction", added Marge. "Indeed, and satisfied patients refer others, and referrals help us attract more affluent patients that will look to us for helping them achieve multiple and more demanding dermatology outcomes." Continued Lou.

Karola chimed in: "and I guess, that higher patient expectations demand personalized treatment plans and contribute to further growing our profit per patient outcome. – A virtuous cycle, if ever there was one."

Dexter summarized the discussion by saying: "Let's periodically re-focus on improving each cog in our flywheel to generate ever accelerating momentum for our business."

As the session wore on, Fletcher steered them towards setting Specific, Transparent, Elevating, and Periodic (S.T.E.P.) Rocks—clear, actionable goals for the upcoming quarter. They needed to be ambitious yet achievable, with clear metrics for success."

The team worked tirelessly into the night, each member dedicated to crafting a strategy that played to their strengths and addressed key business areas. By the end of the second day, they had crafted a comprehensive plan that reimagined DDA's business model, integrated cutting-edge technology, and set clear financial and operational goals.

As they concluded the session, the mood shifted to cautious optimism. Dexter expressed his gratitude: "Thank you, everyone. Your commitment and creativity have turned what could have been the darkest chapter in our history into a blueprint for a bright future. Let's get ready to present this to the private equity group.

We've got a compelling story to tell." Fletcher added, "I'm proud of what we've accomplished here. It's not just the strategy but the unity and determination you've all shown that will convince the investors. Let's make this count."

Leaving the conference room, there was a palpable sense of accomplishment and a renewed belief in their collective strength. They were not just responding to a crisis; they were seizing an opportunity to redefine their future.

Sealing the Future

Dexter Davis, along with Fletcher Henson, stood once again in the imposing conference room of Medical Growth Partners. Today was the culmination of their tireless efforts—a final pitch that could secure the sustained progress of Dexter Davis & Associates. The air was electrical with tension and the gravity of the moment.

Dexter: *(clearing his throat)* "Thank you for giving us the opportunity to revisit our proposal. We've taken your concerns to heart and refined our strategy to not only meet but exceed your expectations."

PE Partner 1: *(skeptically)* "We're listening, Mr. Davis. But as you know, our initial reservations were significant."

Dexter nodded, his resolve firm. Fletcher, stepped forward to unveil their revamped strategy.

Fletcher: "We've developed a comprehensive Strategic Flywheel that integrates proprietary Intellectual Property with a robust set of playbooks. These aren't just operational guidelines; they're the blueprint for scalable, repeatable success across multiple franchises."

PE Partner 2: "Proprietary IP, you say? Explain how this differentiates DDA in the market."

Lou: *(joining in)* "Our team has pioneered a non-invasive diagnostic tool that significantly enhances early detection rates. This tool is not only patented but is also central to our patient care philosophy—better outcomes through better technology."

The partners straightened up now. Dexter felt a shift in the room's energy as Karola detailed the franchise model's merits.

Karola: "The franchise model allows us to expand rapidly without the capital intensity of corporate-run clinics. Each franchisee will operate under stringent guidelines ensuring service quality and brand consistency, powered by our proprietary technology and methods."

PE Partner 3: "And you believe this model will prevent the need for further capital injections?"

Mac: "Absolutely. By leveraging franchising, we significantly reduce our direct investment risk while maintaining control over the brand and clinical standards. It's growth, without diluting our resources or your investment."

The discussion took a technical turn as Dexter and his team elaborated on the financial projections and implementation phases. As they presented, the initial skepticism in the room slowly began to dissipate, replaced by nods of understanding and thoughtful murmurs.

The turning point came unexpectedly. The senior partner of MDP, who had been quiet for most of the meeting, leaned forward, his gaze intense.

Senior Partner: "Your combination of proprietary IP and the strategic use of franchises is compelling. It's an innovative approach to scalability in healthcare. Tell me, Mr. Davis, what are you looking for from us in terms of investment?"

Dexter exchanged a quick glance with Fletcher, a silent agreement passing between them. He knew this was the moment to assert the full value of their revised plan.

Dexter: "We are seeking an investment that recognizes the potential of our model to revolutionize dermatological care. Not just in terms of funding, but a partnership that respects the controlling stake of our management group. We believe in our mission and want to retain the vision that drives DDA."

The room fell silent as the partners deliberated quietly among themselves. After what seemed like an eternity, the senior partner nodded slowly.

Senior Partner: "We're prepared to make that investment, Mr. Davis. Your plan has merit, and we believe in the team you have assembled. Let's discuss the specifics."

As Dexter and Fletcher walked out of the meeting, a sense of relief washed over them. They had done it—they had secured the future of DDA.

oooooooooo

The celebration that evening unfolded at the Dexter Lake House, a picturesque retreat overlooking serene waters under a starlit sky. The entire leadership team gathered, their spirits buoyant and victorious after enduring months of relentless pressure and uncertainty.

Dexter raised his glass, his voice carrying over the gentle lapping of the lake waters. "To a future where DDA sets the standard in dermatological care, where we grow not just in numbers but in the quality of lives we touch. Thank you, each of you, for believing in this vision."

Marge responded with a warm smile, her toast echoing the sentiments of camaraderie that defined the evening. "And to teamwork. We've had our ups and downs, but look at what we've achieved when pulling together."

The air was filled with laughter and chatter as the team reminisced about their journey—the late nights, the brainstorming sessions, and even the occasional disagreements that ultimately strengthened their resolve.

Lou recalled their initial pitches with a mix of humor and humility. "Remember that first meeting with MDP? We were so off the mark it's almost embarrassing."

Karola laughed along, her optimism undimmed by past challenges. "Yes, but look at us now. Adapted, refined, and ready for whatever comes next."

As the evening progressed, the team relaxed by the lakeside, the tension of the past months dissolving into the cool night air. They had not only secured crucial investment but had charted a path forward that promised growth and innovation. More importantly, they had cemented a team dynamic robust enough to withstand future challenges and drive forward with a shared purpose.

Fletcher, always looking ahead, reminded them of the road forward. "This is just the beginning, team. The real work starts now—to implement, to scale, and to lead. But tonight, we celebrate our resilience and our commitment to changing the game."

Under the stars, by the tranquil waters of the lake, Dexter felt a profound gratitude for his team and the journey they had embarked on together. The road ahead was sure to be filled with challenges, but with a team like his, the possibilities were limitless. Tonight, they celebrated not just a financial victory but the spirit of unity and determination that had brought them to this pivotal moment.

Epilogue: A New Horizon

Four years had flown by since Dexter Davis and his team had secured the crucial investment from Medical Growth Partner. Dexter Davis & Associates was now a fixture on the Inc 5000 list, celebrated for its explosive growth and innovation in dermatology.

Tonight, Morgan Jones had organized a grand dinner at Austin's prestigious Jeffrey's restaurant to celebrate DDA's astounding success—three years with revenues multiplied by five and a company value that had septupled.

The restaurant buzzed with excitement as DDA's expanded team of 65 and representatives from 28 franchises mingled, laughter and chatter filling the air. Morgan, ever the charismatic leader, made his way through the crowd, complimenting each team member on their contributions.

Morgan: *(raising his glass)* "Here's to a team that not only dreams big but achieves big! Dexter, your vision has propelled DDA to heights we only imagined. Lou, your technology initiatives have been nothing short of revolutionary."

Lou: *(grinning)* "It's been an incredible ride, Morgan. This team's drive and Dexter's leadership made all the difference. That patent was just the start."

As the evening progressed, Austin's famous DJ, Bingo, set up his decks, turning the formal gathering into a vibrant celebration. Just as the party picked up pace, Morgan discreetly motioned for Dexter and Fletcher to follow him to a private room for a more serious conversation.

Once settled in the dimly lit room, surrounded by the rich aroma of cognac and cigars, Morgan got straight to the point.

Morgan: "Dexter, Fletcher, tonight is not just a celebration. It's also an opportunity. We believe DDA's patented technology has the potential to go global. We're seeing immense interest from affluent markets in the Middle East, Asia, and South America."

Dexter: *(nodding thoughtfully)* "Expanding internationally has always been part of our long-term vision, Morgan. The idea of using our technology through a Telehealth company could redefine access to quality dermatology care worldwide."

Morgan: "Exactly. We envision a network where DDA's non-invasive diagnostics and your trained physicians can provide expert second opinions globally. The scalability of such an initiative could be tremendous."

The discussion then shifted to Fletcher, whose strategic insights had been pivotal in DDA's journey.

Morgan: "Fletcher, your role in this has been crucial. But there's more we'd like to explore. How do you feel about rolling out Summit OS to some of our other portfolio companies? Your methods have proven transformative."

Fletcher: *(pausing to consider)* "I appreciate the confidence, Morgan. I am a licensee of the Summit OS Group, you know, Steve Preda's company. Their mission—to help entrepreneurs reach their ideal lives by creating a positive impact—aligns with what we've accomplished here at DDA."

Morgan: "Preda's personal Why is to eradicate what he calls 'Business Covid' by saving 180,000 SMBs annually speaks volumes. Do you think you could introduce us? Perhaps Steve could also be part of this new venture?"

Fletcher: "I believe that's a conversation worth having. Steve's insights on business growth and sustainability could indeed complement our plans."

As the conversation wrapped up, Morgan proposed a casual yet potentially pivotal meeting.

Morgan: "How about we set up a golf game? You, me, Dexter, and Steve. It would be a great setting to discuss this further."

Fletcher: *(smiling)* "That sounds perfect, Morgan. And it reminds me of the famous quote from the closing scene of Casablanca."

With a chuckle, the three men rejoined the party, their minds buzzing with the possibilities of what lay ahead. The night wound down with a sense of accomplishment and anticipation. DDA had not only navigated its crises, but was now poised to leap onto the global stage, potentially changing the face of dermatology care internationally.

As Dexter looked around at his team, celebrating their collective success, he felt a profound gratitude. This journey had started with a vision to improve patient care, and now, it might just revolutionize an entire industry. Tonight, they celebrated not just what they had achieved but what they were about to embark on—a new chapter that promised even greater challenges and triumphs.

What is Summit OS?

Summit OS® is a business operating system developed by the Summit OS Group that helps you turn your business into a well-oiled machine of growth, profitability and self-management. It is a system that allows you to turn your business into a valuable asset while liberating you from having to run it.

Summit OS Group's Company Why™ is to help entrepreneurs like you reach your Ideal Life while creating a positive impact.

The system is built around the 5 Business Growth Principles™ of People, Purpose, Performance, Playbooks and Profit. Each of these principles can be implemented by mastering the 15 Business Growth Practices™, as explained in the book: *Pinnacle: Five Principles that Take Your Business to the Top of the Mountain*, written by Steve Preda and Gregory Cleary.

You can choose to self-implement Summit OS for your business or for other businesses by becoming a Summit OS Guide™, or you can hire a Guide to implement Summit OS in your business. Learn more by visiting https://SummitOS.co.

The 15 Business Growth Practices

PEOPLE

1. **Culture**: Make sure that everyone in your company lives and breathes the behaviors that have made your best performers help your business to succeed to this point on your journey.

2. **Structure**: Proactively design the right functions with the desired outcomes to move your company forward. Make sure that each such function is owned by the person that can, and wants to drive that function to its maximum impact.

3. **Coaching**: See to it that all your leaders regularly mentor their direct reports, by listening, giving and receiving feedback, and by setting mutual expectations.

PURPOSE

4. **Vision**: Identify the visceral Company Why of your business, the reason it exists, and how it creates a positive impact in the world. Then articulate your "big hairy and audacious" long term goal we call your Summit Vision. This is the north star for your business. Then paint a technicolor vision of the Medium-Term Milestones that your business will have to hit within three years, to be on track to achieving your Summit Vision.

5. **Strategy**: Your strategy is how you will achieve your vision. Identify your Business Constraints™ that drive your brand promises, and the Unique Activities™ that will allow you to build a Strategy Stack and to dig a moat around your business.

6. **Alignment** Align every team member around your Vision and Strategy, so that all your people will understand and internalize where you are going, and how you are going to get there.

PERFORMANCE

10. **Rocks**: Based on your Medium-Term Milestones and Strategy, each year set an Annual Growth Plan™, and execute it in quarterly chunks, we call S.T.E.P. Rocks, the acronym standing for Specific, Transparent, Elevating and Periodic.

11. **Metrics**: Align each of your teammates with your plans by defining Metrics for each person to focus on. Your people will hold each other accountable to achieving these Metrics.

12. **Meetings**: Use meetings to communicate, make decisions, drive action, set priorities, control finances, and strategically plan. Your Meetings should include: Daily Standup-, Weekly Tactical-, and Monthly Financial Meetings and quarterly and annual reviews and planning sessions, respectively.

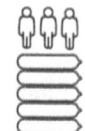

PLAYBOOKS

7. **Define**: Create consistency and scalability in your business by defining the best way of doing things in the form of Playbooks.

8. **Ingrain**: Habitualize your Playbooks by making sure each person that touches them is Trained, Tracked, and Coached until they master their Playbooks and are able to sustain them.

9. **Optimize**: Defining and Ingraining Playbooks is only the start. From there, regularly enrich and simplify every process, as appropriate, and ultimately automate as many of them as possible.

PROFIT

13. **Benchmark**: Profit is the oxygen for growing your business, and you produce profits by adhering to the business growth principles of People, Purpose, Performance and Playbooks. Beyond that, benchmark your profitability to the elite players in your industry, to make sure you grow as fast as the best of them.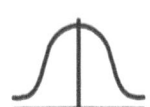

14. **Engineer**: Design your business in such a way to achieve industry leading profitability, and ensure you become and remain a leader in your space.

15. **Sustain**: Maintain your elite profitability by developing a stack of Unique Activities that make you stand apart and near-impossible for your competitors to emulate.

By aligning yourselves around the 5 Business Growth Principles and by implementing the 15 Business Growth Practices, you and your people will row in the same direction and achieve success for your business and the individuals in it.

The Author

Steve Preda's passion is to help eradicate Business Covid, a pandemic killing 180,000 small to medium sized businesses each year in the United States alone.

He built and sold an investment banking firm in his native Hungary before moving to the United States. After arriving, he coached two Vistage CEO peer groups before becoming an EOS Implementer, Scaling Up Coach, and Summit OS Guide™.

Steve is the CEO of Summit OS Group, that developed Summit OS®, an evolution of earlier business operating systems, including E-Myth, EOS, Scaling Up, Jim Collins's work, and others.

Summit OS and its sequel, Strategy OS®, are coherent, customizable, and scalable business operating systems, that allow businesses to grow into Inc 5000 companies and beyond.

Steve and his fellow Summit OS Guides help small to medium-sized businesses Empower their Teams, Execute Like Hell, and Dig a Moat Around their organization to fend off competitors.

Steve has authored six books, including: *Buyable*, *Pinnacle* (with Gregory Cleary), and *Strategy OS*, and he hosts the popular *Management Blueprint®* podcast.

He is a jazz and tennis fan, and lives with his family near Richmond, Virginia.

Check out https://SummitOS.co for details about Summit OS books, blogs and proprietary widgets teaching the 15 Business Growth Practices™, and how you can self-implement Summit OS, Strategy OS, or be matched with an Summit OS Guide, to grow your business.

Summit OS Group Trademarked Terms

10-Method Management™
15 Business Growth Practices™
3x Adventure™
45-Day Execution Momentum™
45-Day Execution™
45-Day Practice Momentum
5 Business Growth Principles™
80:20 Prioritizer™
Activation Handbook™
Advanced Profit per X™
Alignment Accelerators™
Annual Outing™
Automation Activator™
B2B Core Market™
B2C Core Market™
Base Camp Day 1™
Base Camp Day 2™
Base Camp Handbook™
Boost Team Health™
Brainstorming Ground Rules™
Brand Promise Articulator™
Business Constraint™
Business Covid™
Business Expansion Filter™
CEO Check-In Call™
CEO for a Day™
Challenge the Vision™
Climb Accelerators™
Climb Assessment™
Climbing Kit Repair™

Client Clarifier™
Company Why™
Constellation Compass™
Constraint Locator™
Core Business Lens™
Core Value Curator™
Core Value Filter™
Core Value Speech™
Cover Blindspots™
Cross-Functional Playbooks™
Crux Challenge™
Crux Intuitor™
Custom Roadmap™
Customer Journey Playbook™
Customized and Scalable™
Daily Standup Meeting™
Decision-Action Velocity™
Dig a Moat Around Your Business™
DMAIC Improver™
Economy Quadrant™
Eliminate. Automate. Delegate.™
Employee Journey Playbook™
Evaluate the Year™
Execute Like Hell™
Execution Moment™
Execution Momentum™
Execution Planner™
Expansion Dimension™
Expedition Meeting™

Experience Curve Climber™
Flywheel Builder™
Flywheel Themes™
Focus Quadrant™
Friend and Foe Trends™
Function Finder Chart™
Function Outcome™
Function Ownership Chart™
Function Ownership™
Function Owner™
Functional Playbooks™
Give or Earn Trust™
GTM Strategy Grid™
Ideal Life Snake™
Immutable Weaknesses™
Individual Reflections™
Inherent Strengths™
Innovation Actions™
Innovation Culture™
Innovation Driven Business™
Innovation Ideator™
Integrator Myth™
Leaders' Crest™
Leadership Imprints™
Lean Waste Eliminator™
Luxury Quadrant™
M&A Mobilizer™
Management Blueprint®
Medium-Term Milestones™
Meeting Frameworks™
Mentor Meeting Model™
Mentor Meeting™
Milestones Mind-Juggler™
Mindshare Mobilizer™
Mindshare Terms™
Mini CEOs™
Mini CEO™
Momentum Checklist™
Momentum Moment™
Monthly Financial Meeting™
MT Milestones™

Napkin Plan™
Network Effects Catalyzer™
Network Friction Remover™
No Man's Land Map™
Olympian vs. Professional Leader™
Operational Improver™
Optimize Your Playbooks™
Optimizing Tactics™
Output Driven Business™
Peer Accountability™
Playbook Definer™
Playbook Ingrainer™
Playbook Manager™
Playbook Mapping Chart™
Playbook Map™
Playbook Optimizer™
Playbook Ownership Chart™
Playbook Simplifier™
Playbook Toolbox™
Positioning Matrix™
Product Portfolio Map™
Profitability Pine™
Promise to Activity Converter™
Prospect Tracker™
Quarterly Lookout™
Quarterly Mentor Meeting™
Refresh Vision and Strategy™
Reinvention Options™
Response Stimulator™
Roadblock Remover™
Rock-Step Planner™
Rock-Steps™
Rollout Checklist™
S.T.E.P. Rocks™
Scaling Loop Optimizer™
Scaling Loop Selector™
Scoreboard Sketcher™
SEAL Call™
SEAL Camp™
SEAL Slack™

SEAL Summit™
SEALcommerce Store™
Secret CEO Blueprints™
Short Phrase Strategy™
Six Competitive Forces™
Six Dimensions of Expansion™
Six Forces Map™
Sketch 2 Sell™
Smart M&A™
Sprint Rocks™
Starter Toolkit™
Strategic Flywheel™
Strategic Lens Library™
Strategic Position™
Strategy Clarifier™
Strategy Climb Assessment™
Strategy Operating System®
Strategy OS App™
Strategy OS Climb™
Strategy OS Guide™
Strategy OS Spiral™
Strategy OS Toolkit™
Strategy OS®
Strategy Squares™
Strategy Stack™
Subfunction Owner™
Subfunctional Playbooks™
Summit Climb Assessment™
Summit Operating System®
Summit OS App™
Summit OS Climb™
Summit OS Community™
Summit OS Group™
Summit OS Guide™
Summit OS Library™
Summit OS Playbooks™

Summit OS Portal™
Summit OS Toolkit™
Summit OS®
Summit SEAL Team™
Summit Vision™
Tackle Topics™
Talent Assessment Chart™
Team Idea Map™
Tee-up Call™
Tentacle Spreader™
The 11 Business Reinventions™
The 15 Growth Practices™
The 5 Growth Principles™
The 5 Technology Levers™
The 6 Business Levers™
The 7 Smart M&A Approaches™
The 8 Core Business Questions™
The 8 Innovation Catalyzers™
The 8 Waste Eliminators™
The 9 Flywheel Themes™
The Six Sparks™
Topic Tackler™
Unique Activities™
Unique Activity Formulator™
Unique Activity Generator™
Unique Activity Optimizer™
Value and Growth Calculator™
Variety Quadrant™
Vision & Execution Mountain™
Vision & Strategy Map™
Weekly Metrics™
Weekly Tactical Meeting™
WTM Scoreboard™
WTQ Scoreboard™
WTW Scoreboard™
Yin & Yang Leadership™

www.ingramcontent.com/pod-product-compliance
Lightning Source LLC
Chambersburg PA
CBHW021146060526
44107CB00146B/1330/J